Workshop
PanPastel®
by Julia Woning

Amersfoort, 2020

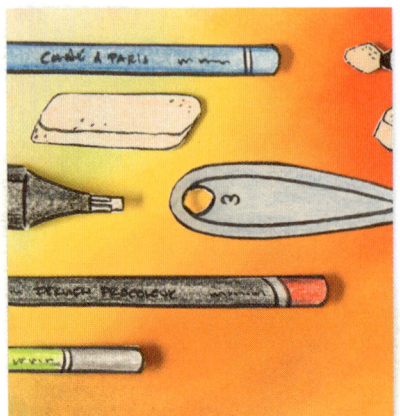
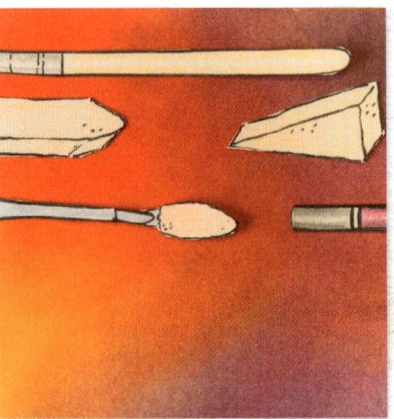
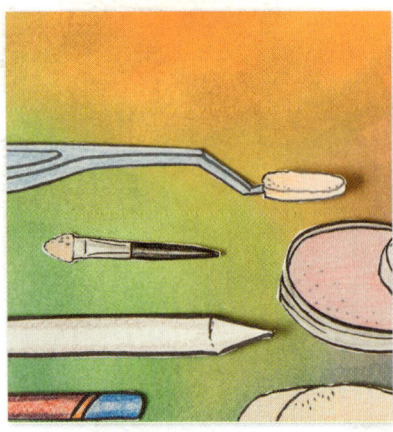
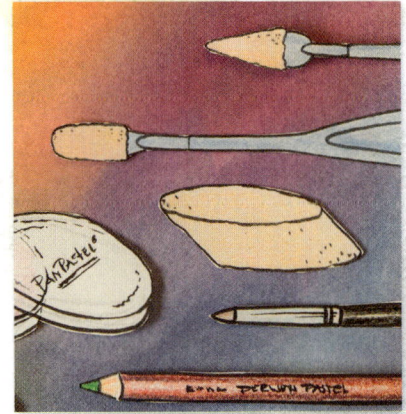

Copyright © 2020 Julia Woning &
BBNC uitgevers bv
Text and illustrations: Julia Woning
Editor: Denise Bos
Layout: BBNC uitgevers bv
Printed in the Czech Republic

MUS is an imprint of
BBNC uitgevers bv

ISBN 978 90 453 2353 4
BISAC ART051000

www.muscreatief.nl
info@bbnc.nl

Attend a PanPastel workshop with
Julia! For available dates and rates,
please visit www.juliawoning.com

TABLE OF CONTENTS

FOREWORD	05
HISTORY OF PANPASTEL	06
THE DIFFERENCE BETWEEN PASTEL STICKS AND PANPASTEL	08
PANPASTEL VERSUS PASTEL STICKS	09
PANPASTEL COLOUR RANGE	10
SOFFT TOOLS	12
USING PASTEL PENCILS AND COLOURED PENCILS	18
BLACK AND WHITE PANPASTEL	22
PROJECT: BLACK AND WHITE COLOURING PAGE	24
PROJECT: BLACK AND WHITE LION	26
PROJECT: BLACK AND WHITE FOREST PATH	28
PROJECT: BLACK AND WHITE PORTRAIT	32
TIME FOR COLOUR	36
TRANSFER TECHNIQUES WITH PANPASTEL	40
USING PANPASTEL WITH STENCILS	41
PROJECT: POSTCARDS	42
PROJECT: LABEL	44
PROJECT: ART JOURNAL PAGE WITH BIRDS	48
PROJECT: ART JOURNAL PAGE WITH LOVELY LADY	50
PROJECT: COLOURING PAGE	52
PROJECT: GREYSCALE	54
PROJECT: SKETCHES	58
PROJECT: TULIP IN PRIMARY COLOURS	60
PROJECT: PAINTING OUTDOORS	64
SKIN TONES	66
PROJECT: PORTRAIT IN COLOUR	70
PROJECT: COW	74
PROJECT: GOLDFISH	76
PROJECT: LANDSCAPE	78
PROJECT: EYE ON CANVAS	82
PROJECT: PORTRAIT ON LARGE CANVAS	86
PROJECT: ABSTRACT ON CANVAS	88
PROJECT: SCULPTURE BLOCKS	92
PROJECT: ENCAUSTIC MEDIUM	94
ACKNOWLEDGEMENTS	96

PANPASTEL: A UNIQUE & VERSATILE MEDIUM WITH MANY POSSIBLE USES!

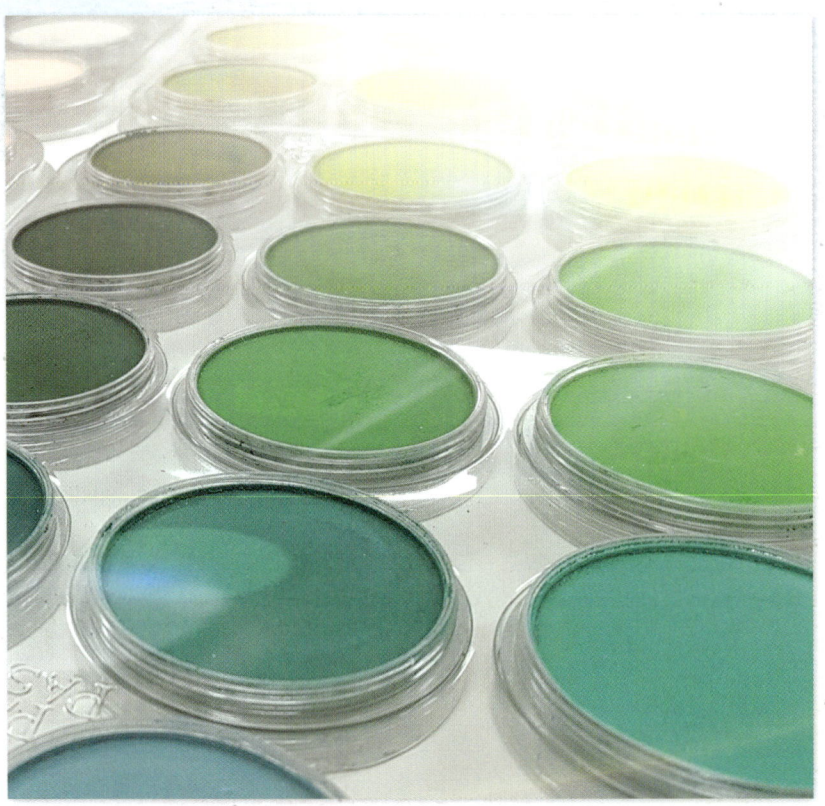

FOR NEW DRAWING & PAINTING TECHNIQUES

I would like to introduce myself: my name is Julia Woning. I graduated from the Willem de Kooning Academy in 1994 and have been working as an illustrator, portraitist and visual artist ever since. I work from my studio in Bergschenhoek, South Holland. I am always drawing and creating. Since 2015, I have been making colouring books for MUS with my famous "Lovely Ladies" and animal illustrations. Following two beautiful reference books on colouring materials and colouring techniques (Colouring Techniques Workshop and Creative Drawing Techniques Workshop), we now have this special book about PanPastel®.

PanPastel is a versatile new material. It is actually a kind of dry paint that you can use in a variety of different ways. I love to use this product in my work and this book is intended to demonstrate its many possibilities. I hope that I can inspire you to start using this fantastic medium and to also help you to make beautiful creations. I wish you many hours of informative study, and above all a lot of fun with this book.

Julia

Note: If you are interested in attending one of my workshops please visit www.juliawoning.com for details of the various workshops, rates and workshop dates.

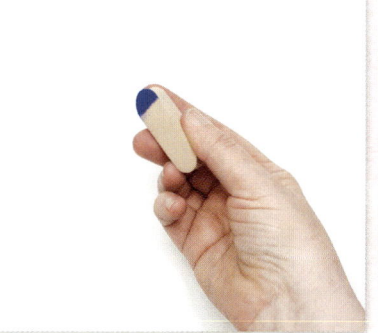

HISTORY OF PANPASTEL

PanPastel® was created by Colorfin, a company that develops, produces and sells new materials for artists. Colorfin's founders Ladd Forsline and Bernadette Ward have both been working in the artists' materials industry since the late 1980s. Ladd is an artist and the inventor of, among other things, OilBar® (oil paint in stick form) and Colour Shaper® (brushes with silicone tips). Bernadette has many years of experience in management, marketing and product development, in the field of artists' materials and other consumer products.

The idea behind the development of PanPastel was to create a dry colour medium that would work like a fluid paint. Bernadette & Ladd saw that the pastel medium hadn't changed from the stick format for hundreds of years; and before that, going back thousands of years, humans had used natural raw pigments to draw and paint (as seen at the Lascaux Caves).

For centuries the pastel medium has only been available in the format that we still know and use: pastel sticks. Since the development of pastel sticks, nothing has changed in the appearance and basic formula of sticks for centuries. Yet the pastel stick format does have some limitations. Ladd and Bernadette noticed that there was a kind of love-hate relationship for sticks between artists who used painting (wet) mediums and those who used pastel sticks (dry medium).

So, they wanted to create a product that took advantage of all the characteristics of the pastel medium that everyone loves – it's directness and purity of colour – plus offer new characteristics (such as the ability to mix colors and control transparency) to eliminate some of the limitations. Making a product that all artists could love.

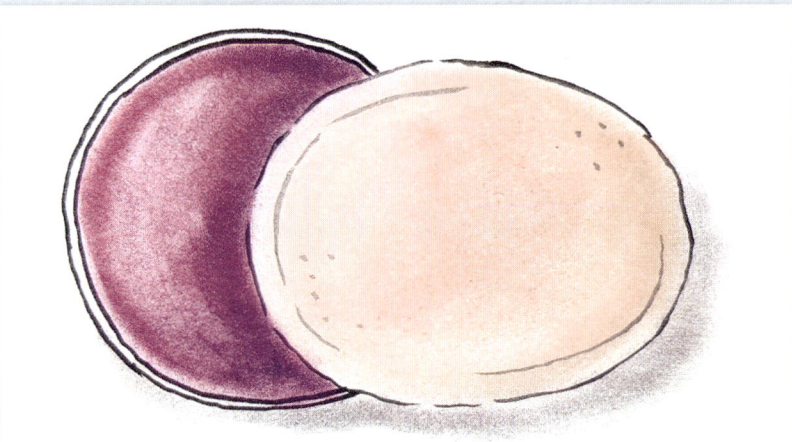

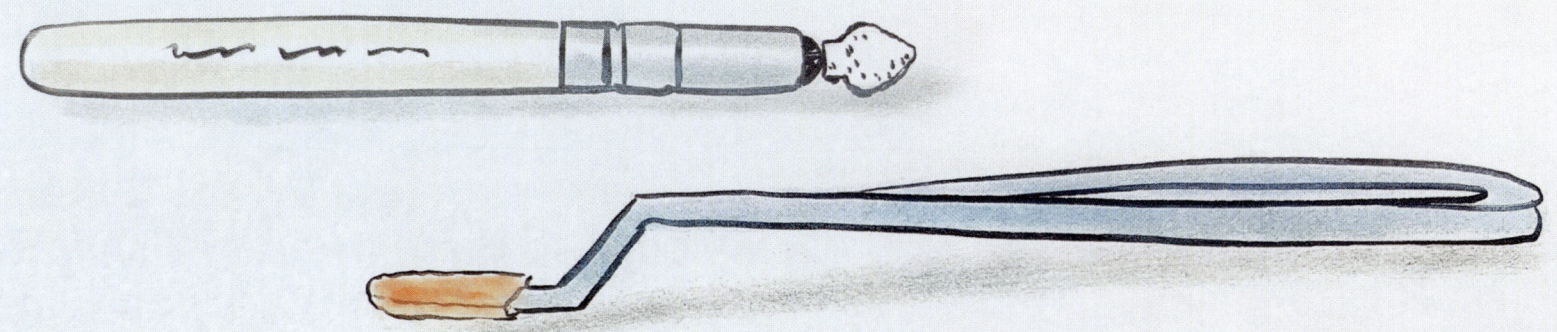

After 5 years and much experimentation they developed the pan format, filled with their proprietary pastel formulations to create a cake-like format, creating PanPastel®.

PanPastel's range includes eighty "original" colours. In addition, six metallic colours, six pearlescent colours and five mediums (including a Colorless Blender) are also available. PanPastel Colours are independently tested for lightfastness using the ASTM (American Society for Testing and Materials) standard – an objective way to measure lightfastness.

PanPastel is exclusively manufactured from the highest quality artist's pigments, with the minimum possible use of binders and fillers. The result is a high concentration of pigment, and an ultra-soft consistency that minimises dust when applied with the micropore sponge based Sofft Tools. Each PanPastel pan has a diameter of 6 cm (2.4") – the size is the optimum size to work with all of the different applicator sizes – making it easy to use the large sponges for underpaintings and blocking-in as well as the smaller applicators for painting & drawing. And it gives the best value to the artist by offering a high volume of colour.

Colorfin also developed Sofft Tools – these are tools developed to facilitate the use of PanPastel. Sofft Tools are applicators made from a special micropore sponge.

Since their company was founded, Ladd and Bernadette have won several awards for the products they created.

Full information along with videos and other resources available at: PanPastel.com.

ITS UNIQUE PAN FORMAT ENABLES PANPASTEL TO BE USED LIKE A PAINT

THE DIFFERENCE BETWEEN PASTEL STICKS AND PANPASTEL

Pastel sticks are made with pigment and a binder / kaolin (clay), which can be used to make drawings in a manner similar to painting. The 'pastel' in the name may suggest that only pale pastel tints are available, but pastel stick ranges include mass tones (pure colours), which are tinted with white to produce light tints. And black to create darker shades. As a result, a very wide range of colours is available. The pastel medium has been in use since the 15th century. It was mainly used to create preliminary sketches for large oil paintings. Leonardo da Vinci was one of the first recorded artists to use pastel sticks. It was a widely used material in portraiture by around the 18th century. Pastel sticks are widely used today by both realistic and abstract artists: you can use it to create layer upon beautiful layer, as long as the working surface or paper has enough 'tooth' to hold the multiple layers. Pastel sticks are opaque and can generate dust: which can give your work a velvety appearance.

PanPastel was launched in 2007: it offers a completely new way to use the pastel medium. Although PanPastel is a true pastel, its pan

PANPASTEL'S UNIQUE PROPERTIES MEAN THE PASTEL MEDIUM CAN BE USED IN NEW WAYS

format gives it a range of unique properties. PanPastel doesn't replace pastel sticks, as they work differently. On the right, you will find a list of the attributes that set it apart from classic pastel sticks.

PANPASTEL VERSUS PASTEL STICKS

- PANPASTEL GENERATES CONSIDERABLY LESS DUST THAN PASTEL STICKS.
- YOU CAN WORK MUCH MORE ECONOMICALLY WITH PANPASTEL COMPARED TO PASTEL STICKS. EACH PAN OF COLOUR LASTS LONGER AND THERE IS LESS WASTE.
- UNLIKE WITH PASTEL STICKS, PANPASTEL COLOURS CAN BE EASILY MIXED, LIKE PAINT, TO CREATE AN INFINITE PALETTE OF COLOURS.
- PANPASTEL HAS SUPERIOR ADHESIVE CHARACTERISTICS COMPARED TO PASTEL STICKS, ENABLING YOU TO WORK ON A BROADER RANGE OF WORKING SURFACES - FROM SMOOTH TO TEXTURED.
- ALTHOUGH PANPASTEL OFFERS EXCELLENT ADHESION, IT IS ALSO EASIER TO ERASE THAN PASTEL STICKS, USING ANY ERASER, MAKING IT A VERY FORGIVING MEDIUM.
- BOTH PANPASTEL AND PASTEL STICKS CAN BE APPLIED LAYER UPON LAYER. THE LAYERS CAN BE ISOLATED WITH A PASTEL FIXATIVE PRIOR TO APPLYING THE NEXT LAYER.
- ANOTHER IMPORTANT CHARACTERISTIC OF PANPASTEL IS THAT IT IS VERY MIXED MEDIA FRIENDLY. FOR EXAMPLE WITH PASTEL STICKS AND COLOURED PENCILS (BOTH WAX AND OIL) ALONG WITH MOST OTHER ARTIST'S MEDIA.
- MY TIPS: START WORKING AS IF YOU WERE PAINTING WITH WATERCOLOURS. WORK BY BLOCKING-IN SOME AREAS OF PANPASTEL COLOUR, OMITTING OTHER AREAS, OR ERASING INTO THE PANPASTEL UNDERPAINTING FOR A SUBTRACTIVE EFFECT. USE YOUR PANPASTEL AS A BASE LAYER AND YOUR PASTEL STICKS TO CREATE ACCENTS. IF YOU REMEMBER TO DO THIS, YOU WON'T NEED TO USE ANYTHING ELSE.

The PanPastel range of colours

As I mentioned earlier, the PanPastel colour range comprises eighty colours. The range includes:

- 20 **Pure** Colours
- 20 **Tints** – pure colours mixed with white
- 20 **Shades** – pure colours mixed with black
- 20 **Extra Darks** – pure colours mixed with even more black

In addition to these eighty colours, there are also six metallic colours, six pearlescent colours and five mediums on the market, all of which are available in the pan format. All the colours can be found on the next page. The colours are available individually and they can also be threaded together to form a tower, use a lid on the top to protect that colour.

A Palette Tray is available to hold the individual pans, where the colours can be placed securely. This creates a painter's palette, as it were. A selection of pre-selected sets of colours are available. Including sets with the full range of colours in palette trays.

Palette Trays are available to hold the pans

SOFFT TOOLS

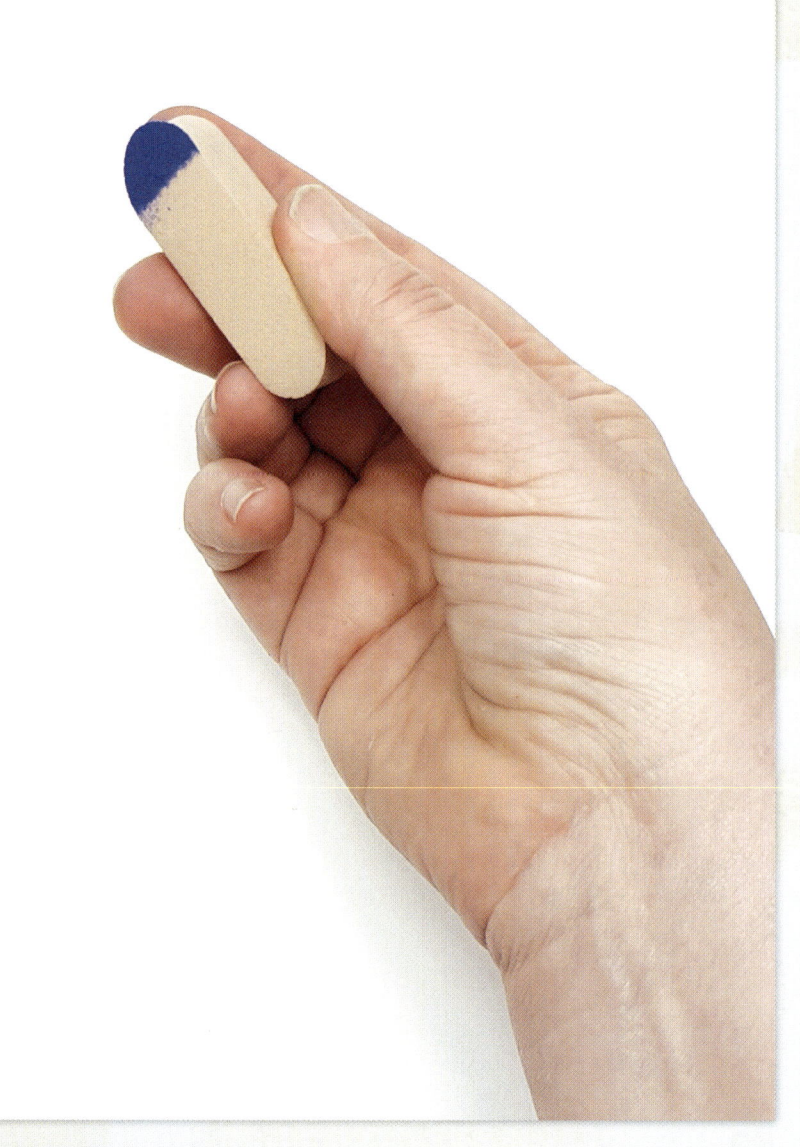

Colorfin developed Sofft Tools to enable the optimum application of PanPastel. These are made from a proprietary micropore sponge and are available in different shapes, resembling artist's brush shapes: oval, round, point and flat. These sponges are the thickness of your finger and are easy to hold. There are also larger sponges, which make blocking-in larger areas very easy. This works much easier than if you want to colour large areas with traditional pastel sticks. Sofft Knives are also available for details and small areas. They look like a palette knife, with a kind of sponge sleeve (cover). These covers can be changed if the sponge is dirty or worn. These Sofft Knives are available in four different varieties: with oval, round, point and flat shapes. Sofft applicators are also available in addition to the tools. These are similar to a pencil, but with a sponge attachment. This allows you to work even more precisely and finely. You can of course switch to pastel pencils for very fine lines and accents.

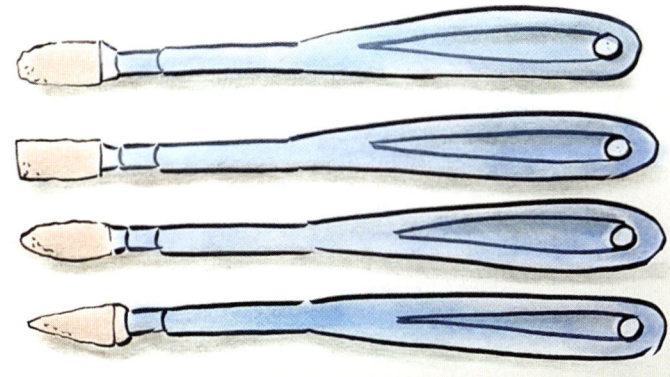

SOFFT TOOLS ARE AVAILABLE IN DIFFERENT SHAPES

You can easily load Sofft Tools with PanPastel Colour. You do not have to apply great force to transfer colour to your tool; just a couple of swipes across the pan's surface is sufficient to load the Sofft Tool with colour.

Swiping the pan's surface more than necessary will generate excess dust. This is not required – just carefully pick it up with your tool in order to load it. Always keep in mind that loading your tool or sponge with colour can be done in just one or two gentle swipes, there really is no need to generate excess dust!

One more thing: colours can be easily mixed, either on the pan's surface or on your working surface. You can create orange by just swiping a little red onto your yellow pans and mixing it there. Afterwards, wipe off the

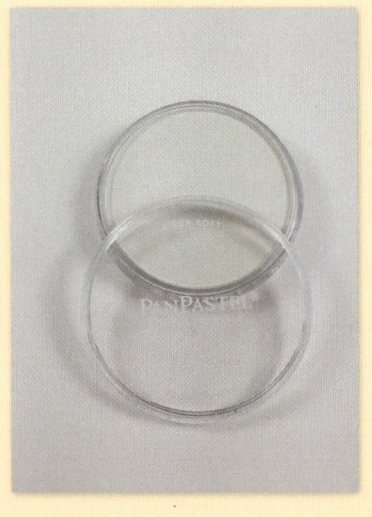

THE PANPASTEL COLORLESS BLENDER IS INDISPENSABLE WHEN USING PANPASTEL. TO ME, IT IS MORE THAN JUST A TOOL TO BLEND MY PANPASTEL. IT IS ALSO AN EXTREMELY USEFUL MATERIAL: I FIND IT HELPS PRESERVE MY SOFFT TOOLS. WHEN YOU APPLY MORE PANPASTEL TO "TOOTHY" PASTEL PAPER, SUCH AS MI-TEINTES TOUCH OR PASTELMAT, THE COLORLESS BLENDER CAN REDUCE THE WEAR ON YOUR TOOLS. THIS BOOK CONTAINS EXERCISES WITH AND WITHOUT THE USE OF A COLORLESS BLENDER. SO YOU CAN EXPERIENCE THE DIFFERENCES FOR YOURSELF.

red from your yellow pans with a clean sponge or paper towel. You could also mix your colours on a separate piece of paper before applying them to your working surface. Personally, I prefer to use my big sponge as a kind of palette. For example, I mix yellow and red on my sponge, and then apply it to my drawing. To wipe your Knife with Cover clean, swipe left to right over a piece of paper (kitchen) towel. If you swipe from front to back, the Cover may slip off the Knife. If one side of the sleeve is dirty or damaged, simply turn it around. In addition to the flat sides of the sponge, use its tip and edges.

The picture shown on the next page demonstrates how you can use all sides of the tool in one single movement. Try out different marks yourself in the adjacent boxes. Also, try varying the pressure you use for different effects.

Try out the tools here with different lines and strokes.

SPONGES CAN BE CLEANED BETWEEN COLOURS ON A PAPER TOWEL

Loading your tool with colour

During the intermediate step of mixing colours on a large sponge, you will learn to use the exact amount of PanPastel that you need in order to get the desired colour. Practice mixing to become familiar with using and mixing PanPastel, but you will find that you will develop a feel for it soon enough. Before you know it, you will be mixing the most radiant orange colours by adding a little yellow and red, and also try with a little Colorless Blender.

Cleaning the sponges

Dirty sponges can be easily cleaned simply by wiping them on a paper (kitchen) towel. Thus switching from one colour to another is easily done – just wipe, and your tool is ready for the next colour. But you can reduce cleaning time by using different tools for different colour groups, or for light and for dark colours. Every now and then you may want to wash the tools – simply use warm water with a mild detergent. Allow to air dry fully. Always carefully remove the sleeves from your palette knife – and especially when you slide them back on – to prevent tearing.

Using alternative tools to apply PanPastel

Although the original tools work best for me, you are of course free to try alternative materials to apply PanPastel Colours. Using your fingers to apply or remove colour is not recommended. On the other hand, using brushes is okay. However the brush bristles tend to create extra dust, whereas PanPastel is a low dust medium. Of course, this need not become a major problem, so experiment with what you have available! Another option is to use alternative sponges. This is fine, but the Sofft Tools micropore formulation so exquisitely complements PanPastel that I still believe the original Sofft Tool Sponges & Applicators work the best.

Which working surface?

PanPastel is a versatile medium that can be used on a wide variety of surfaces, such as drawing paper, textured pastel paper or on canvas. Another extremely useful quality of PanPastel is that it can also be used over acrylic paint, modelling paste and other mediums that you have applied as a ground on your canvas. In the pictures shown alongside, you can see how PanPastel adheres to different surfaces, both paper and other mediums.

TRY OUT A VARIETY OF SURFACES & GROUNDS

USING PASTEL PENCILS AND COLOURED PENCILS

When using pastel sticks, it is normal practice to use a pastel pencil to add in the details. Depending on how well your working surface and the pencil work together, you can use it to make fine lines in your pastel drawing. However, pastel sticks tend to flood the tooth of the surface quickly, making it difficult to work on top of it with a pastel pencil. With a little time and practice, you will understand when you can use a pencil over your sticks and when not to, but as stated before, this is something you will learn with time and practice. With PanPastel however, it is very easy to use coloured pencils for lines and details, even after several layers. The pencil seems to adhere better to PanPastel than to pastel sticks. Coloured pencils can also be used on PanPastel, but not on pastel sticks; the wax or oil of the pencil does not go well with the powder of pastel sticks. You can easily apply colour with a coloured pencil over a thin layer of PanPastel. To increase adhesion and to improve the results with pastel pencils, you can fix both pastel sticks and PanPastel with a pastel fixative at intermediate stages. When fixing, it is recommended to build up light layers and to always spray outside or in a well ventilated area. Make sure you use a good fixative. Don't use a cheap fixative (and definitely no hairspray!), because it can yellow or become sticky over time. So you can protect your work, if desired, with a good quality spray pastel fixative for intermediate and final layers.

PRACTICE TO GET A FEEL FOR HOW THE DIFFERENT MEDIUMS WORK TOGETHER

Try out how the mediums work in these boxes. Use pastel sticks with pastel pencil, and pastel sticks with coloured pencil, and vary the number and thickness of the pastel stick layers that you put on paper before you use a pencil over them. Apply your PanPastel in the other boxes and vary the amount there as well. Discover the differences when you put your pencil on top of them.

In the project below, I used coloured pencil over PanPastel.

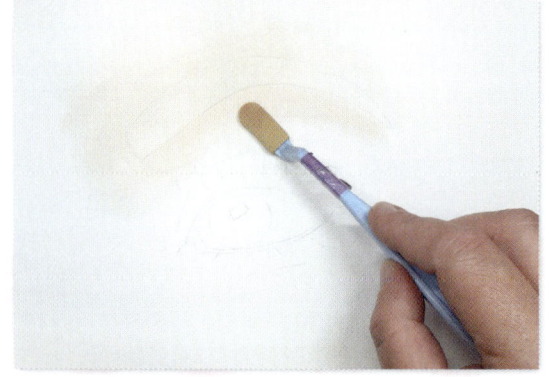
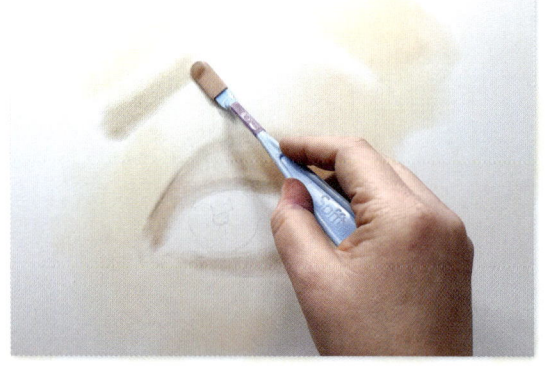

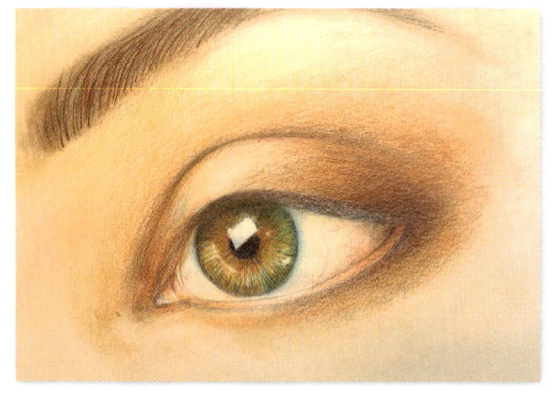

I sketched the eye on 225 grams of Schut Artist Drawing Paper. I started with PanPastel skin tones and then I added many layers of coloured pencils, in this case Derwent Procolour pencils. On the next page, you will find a line drawing of an eye that you can colour in with PanPastel. Apply thin layers of PanPastel Colour so that the coloured pencil will adhere well.

BLACK AND WHITE PANPASTEL

Now it's time for the real PanPastel work! Let's start with just black and white.

The following exercises will help you discover the differences between working with and without the Colorless Blender, and will allow you to explore which method you prefer. First, practice on the smooth paper shown opposite, and then try the same exercise on Pastelmat® or another textured pastel paper, so that you can also experience different types of paper. Don't forget that the textured paper "grabs" more colour in order for it to "flow" properly. Don't be too heavy handed, to minimise the wear and tear on your sponges. Notice that the colors look different on textured papers compared to smooth papers.

TRY LOADING YOUR SOFFT TOOL WITH TWO COLOURS

- CREATE A GRADATION FROM WHITE PAPER TO BLACK PANPASTEL WITH COLORLESS BLENDER

- CREATE A GRADATION FROM WHITE PANPASTEL TO BLACK PANPASTEL WITHOUT COLORLESS BLENDER

- CREATE A GRADATION FROM WHITE PANPASTEL TO BLACK PANPASTEL WITH COLORLESS BLENDER

Paste your other test papers below

PROJECT:

BLACK AND WHITE COLOURING PAGE

Here is a colouring page from my Colourful Peoples of the World colouring book, coloured with black and white PanPastel. I used the Colorless Blender to further enhance colour mixing. Another image from the colouring book is shown opposite. Try to colour it with only black and white.

PROJECT:
BLACK AND WHITE LION

PanPastel is also excellent for sketching

You will achieve quick results, which makes it highly suitable for studies. In this example, I have sketched a lion on anthracite coloured Pastelmat paper. I mainly used white, so I could fully exploit the dark background. In the final layers, I increased the contrast from light to dark by creating the dark parts with black PanPastel. These few accents complete my sketch of the lion's head. When I sketch, I work alternately with a Sofft Sponge and various other Sofft Tools to achieve exactly what I need. Don't be afraid to explore and find out what really works best for you!

PROJECT:

BLACK AND WHITE FOREST PATH

If you find it difficult to draw, this exercise is very good to try. To transfer a sketch to the Pastelmat paper I use a gridded drawing system: I place my photo in a transparent card with a grid of small squares on it (drawing grid). I lightly draw these squares on my paper, then I draw what I see in each square. This way you can enlarge your photo, but still render it in the right proportions on your Pastelmat. I opted for a dark paper colour, which clearly shows that you are using black and white. When my sketch was transferred to the paper, I started with white PanPastel. I always work from the background to the foreground. With this picture, I really wanted to catch the natural light, so I applied a lot of white. You can see that between the trees and in other places where white space is required, I have applied more opaque areas of white.

I MAKE A SKETCH USING A GRIDDED DRAWING SYSTEM

After that I slowly build up the layers of colour increasing the darker colours with soft shades of grey. You can also see that I worked from large shapes to small; I started by blocking-in the larger areas of the trees then adding an increasing number of details with the smaller tools. When I was satisfied with the contrast, I added some extra accents with a white pastel pencil. Pastel pencils work very well on Pastelmat paper, especially if it already has a number of layers of PanPastel on it. I applied a little more black in a couple of areas. The best thing about the Flat (No.2) Sofft Knife is that you can also use the edge of the shape. As shown in the images I used it for highlighting dark leaves. Finally, I added some white accents to the blades of grass. Now it's ready!

DO NOT FORGET TO WORK:

* FROM BACKGROUND TO FOREGROUND
* FROM TOP TO BOTTOM
* FROM LARGE SHAPES TO SMALL

PROJECT:

BLACK AND WHITE PORTRAIT

For this project I painted a portrait with PanPastel and pastel pencils. I made a sketch on Pastelmat paper, then I blocked-in large areas with a sponge and a light grey colour. Building up a number of layers to create a gentle gradation. After I applied the base layers for the face, I used my tools to create the smaller areas of colour. With a dark grey colour, I applied shading to the face. I also used some darker colours around the eyes. With PanPastel I further worked out the eyes, nose and mouth. I applied the final details with pastel pencils to add the finishing touches that will add power to your portrait..

BUILD UP PLENTY OF LAYERS

I USE PASTEL PENCILS TO APPLY THE FINAL DETAILS

Even with many layers of PanPastel on the paper, you can still easily use pastel pencils. I did that for the eyelashes for example. When I was satisfied with the face, I began working on the hair. I first blocked-in the large areas with a sponge and then used a smaller Sofft Tool to add the strands of hair. I drew individual hairs using a pastel pencil, giving the portrait an even more realistic look. I used different brands of pastel pencils for both the dark and light grey tones: Derwent, Stabilo CarbOthello, Conté à Paris and Caran d'Ache.

NOW IT'S TIME TO TURN OUR ATTENTION TO COLOUR

I would like to show you how easily you can mix colours with PanPastel. Let's start by creating a gradation with a pure red colour as we did with the black and white exercise on page 23.

- CREATE A GRADATION GOING FROM WHITE PAPER TO RED PANPASTEL WITHOUT THE COLORLESS BLENDER

- CREATE A GRADATION GOING FROM WHITE PAPER TO RED PANPASTEL WITH THE COLORLESS BLENDER

- CREATE A GRADATION GOING FROM WHITE PANPASTEL TO RED PANPASTEL WITHOUT THE COLORLESS BLENDER

JULIA'S FAVOURITE PALETTE OF COLOURS. AVAILABLE INDIVIDUALLY OR AS A KIT.

My basic palette of PanPastel colours is shown in the image. I made this combination from the 80 original colours plus a Colorless Blender, with which you can mix a large variety of colours. My basic colours are yellow, warm red, cool red, cool blue, warm blue, white, black, grey and a skin tone. The colour numbers I use are: 220.5 Hansa Yellow, 340.5 Permanent Red, 430.5 Magenta, 580.5 Turquoise, 520.5 Ultramarine Blue, 100.5 Titanium White, 800.5 Black, 820.2 Neutral Grey Extra Dark, 740.8 Burnt Sienna Tint and the 010 Colorless Blender. I can mix the following colours to generate gradations.

580.5 TURQUOISE — 220.5 HANSA YELLOW   220.5 HANSA YELLOW — 520.5 ULTRAMARINE BLUE

430.5 MAGENTA — 220.5 HANSA YELLOW   220.5 HANSA YELLOW — 340.5 PERMANENT RED

430.5 MAGENTA — 580.5 TURQUOISE   520.5 ULTRAMARINE BLUE — 340.5 PERMANENT RED

COOL COLOURS

WARM COLOURS

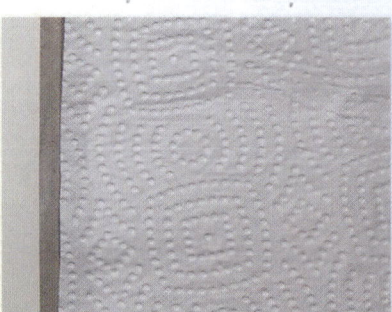

In this example, I have used yellow, red and blue to fill in a cool version of Johannes Itten's colour wheel. Apply colour to the colour wheel shown opposite, by mixing the three colours. Also load your Sofft Tool regularly, so you get a feel for the amount of PanPastel you need to mix a colour. Also try mixing on your large sponge, and using that as a palette. As these are high quality artists' pigments, each pigment has unique characteristics and therefore the amount of colour required will vary from pigment to pigment. Once you are comfortable with the amount of colour on your tool, continue with the other colours. Create another colour wheel for yourself in a warm version.

PANPASTEL FOR TRANSFER TECHNIQUES

The good adhesion of PanPastel makes it perfectly suitable for making your own transfer. You can use all of the colours and make transfers on many different surfaces. Apply a good layer of PanPastel on the back of your sketch or photocopy. Then place it on a piece of paper or canvas and trace the lines to transfer the image or sketch. This technique is very fast and is also easy to erase. Try it!

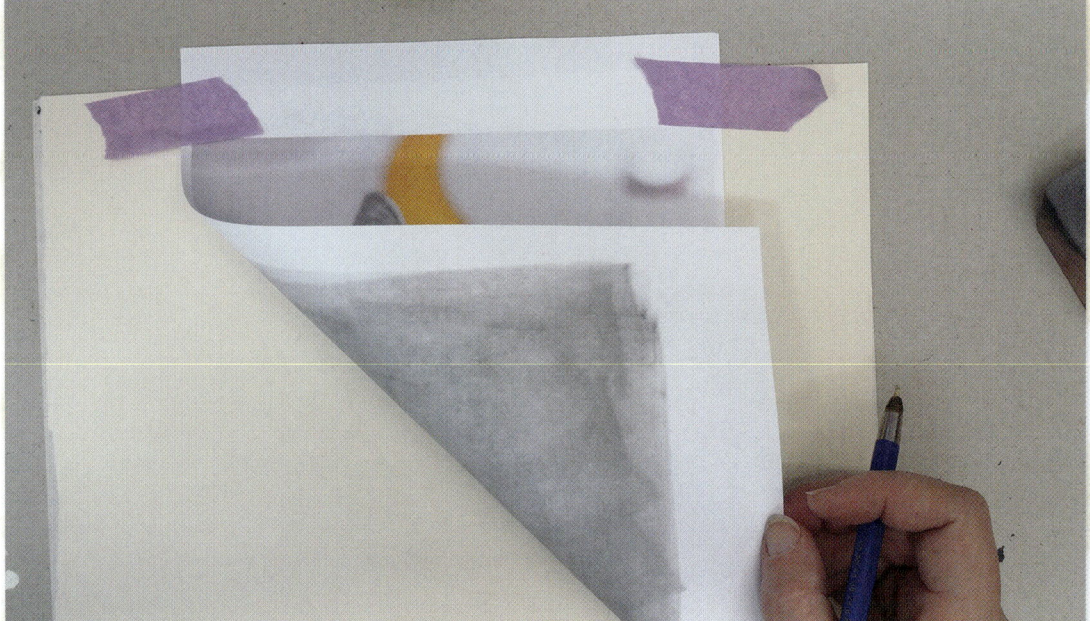

PanPastel and Stencils

THERE ARE SEVERAL TECHNIQUES FOR COMBINING THE USE OF PANPASTEL WITH STENCILS. YOU CAN SIMPLY APPLY THE COLOUR OVER YOUR STENCIL PATTERN WITH A DABBING MOTION. MAKE SURE YOU DON'T PUSH PANPASTEL UNDER THE STENCIL.

YOU CAN ALSO USE A VERSAMARK© WATERMARK (CLEAR) INK PAD. APPLY THE INK OVER YOUR STENCIL WITH A DABBING MOTION USING A SPONGE. BE CAREFUL NOT TO USE TOO MUCH! ALLOW THE CLEAR INK TO DRY A LITTLE AND THEN USE A SOFFT TOOL TO DAB ON A LITTLE PANPASTEL COLOUR. YOU CAN REMOVE THE STENCIL AFTER APPLYING THE LAYER OF INK, OR ELSE YOU CAN LEAVE IT IN PLACE UNTIL YOU HAVE FINISHED APPLYING COLOUR.

THIS TECHNIQUE CAN BE USED ON ALL TYPES OF SURFACES: POSTCARDS, COLOURING PAGES, LABELS, ART JOURNALS OR ON A DRAWING, TO GIVE IT MORE DIMENSION. BUT YOU CAN ALSO USE IT ON PAINTINGS OR SCULPTURES. THE POSSIBILITIES ARE ENDLESS.

PROJECT: POSTCARD

In this project I will show how you can make a postcard by building up a layered image using different stencils. In this example, I have used 225 grams Schut Artist Drawing Paper, but many other kinds of paper can also be used. Just try out various types and brands of paper to find out which one you like best.
I started by applying the background. For this I used PanPastel Colours and the Colorless Blender; apply light layers of PanPastel and blend. Then using the first stencil, I applied the lightest colour. The rule is: the farther away, the lighter the colour. This adds greater depth to your image. I then carefully dabbed on the PanPastel. Make sure you don't push colour under the stencil. Before applying the next layer, fix the previous layer using pastel fixative. You can now continue with the second stencil. To get a beautiful effect, I used a VersaMark ink pad combined with a sponge.

FIX YOUR INTERMEDIATE LAYERS WITH PASTEL FIXATIVE

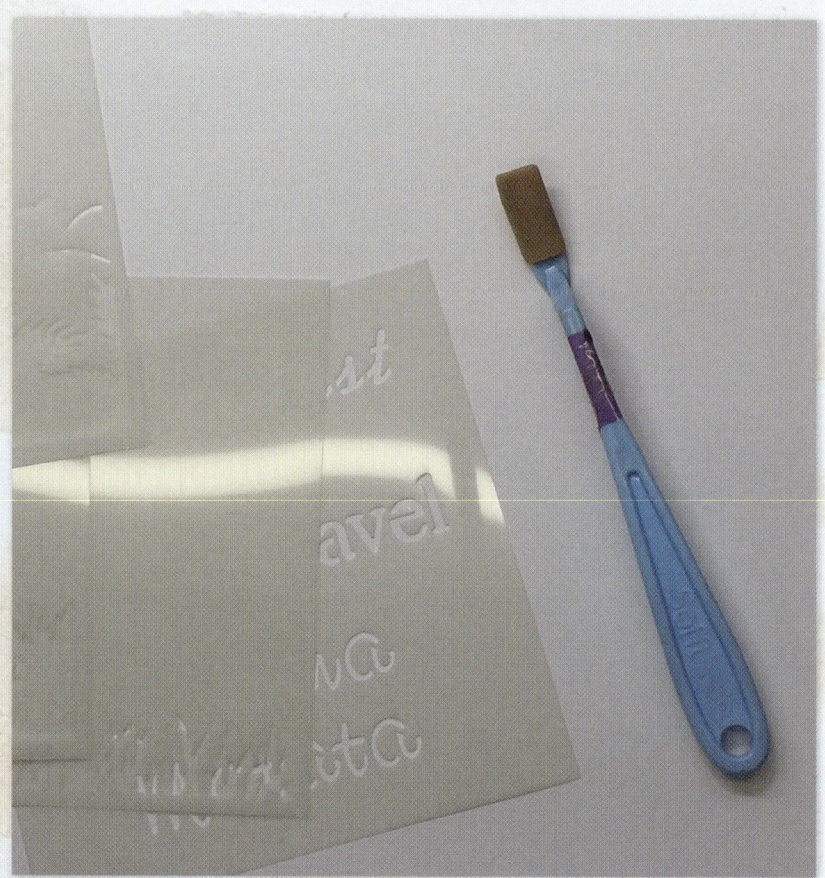

I applied a thin layer of ink, then put the stencil aside, then applied a dark PanPastel colour on top of it. That way I didn't get a dark colour in my previous lighter layer. You can see that I used several dark shades, which gave the postcard more dimension. I repeated this step with the third stencil, only this time, I used an even darker colour. You can enhance the effect of depth if you create a good contrast from light to dark.

PROJECT:
LABEL

Give your gifts a personal touch with a handmade label. Labels are also very nice small projects! I created the label's background for this project using two colours and a little Colorless Blender. I used a stencil on my background. I removed a little of the PanPastel in different areas using a kneaded eraser, to create a dot pattern. Using the stencil, I then applied darker dots with my Sofft Tool. The pictures show the light dots as well as the overlapping dark dots. When I was satisfied with the colours and the pattern, I fixed the background, to protect it from getting smudged.

In this project, I will show you the contrast you can create using an ink pad. I used a VersaMark pad. I applied the VersaMark on a new stencil using the stamp pad itself. After it had dried a bit, I lightly dabbed PanPastel over the inked area. You could also first remove the stencil before applying the colour, but my personal preference is to leave the stencil in place and apply the colour over it. After applying a sufficient amount of colour, I removed the stencil and was able to clearly see the print. I repeated these steps in various places on the label. I wanted to make a festive label,

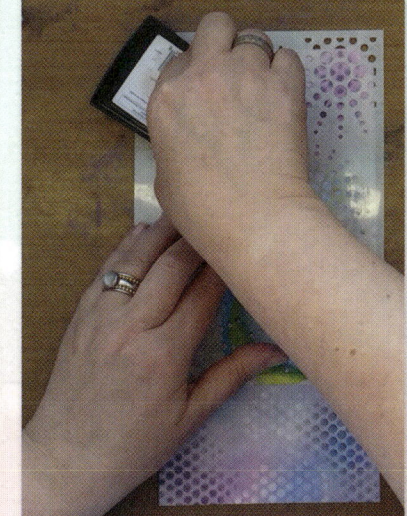

so I chose text to match. I used a graphite pencil to write the text, after which I used a VersaMark pen over it. This allows you to create thinner and more specific lines. After the VersaMark had dried a little, I dabbed on different PanPastel colours. I then

removed the excess PanPastel with a kneaded eraser, after the ink had dried fully. This makes the letters look a little sharper. I hung the finished label on the present for the birthday person.

INK PADS & STAMPS CAN BE USED TO CREATE STRONGER CONTRASTS

PROJECT:
ART JOURNAL PAGE WITH BIRDS

PanPastel is excellent for use in your art journal. I created a page with birds, starting with a cloudy background using different PanPastel colours. I fixed the background after I was satisfied with it. With my self-designed foam stamp from Pronty Crafts by Julia Woning, which I fully loaded with a VersaMark ink pad, I stamped the page full of leaves. I then applied various PanPastel Colours to the inked areas. The leaves gradually began to appear!

I also fixed this layer with a pastel fixative. I then used other stamps from my collection to stamp ink birds on the page. I created greater depth by overlapping the images and stamping a few leaves and twigs over the birds in various places. After the ink was dry, I coloured the birds with PanPastel and then fixed the page one last time.

YOU CAN CREATE DEPTH BY OVERLAPPING IMAGES

I WILL START WITH THE BACKGROUND AND WILL THEN FIX IT

PROJECT:
ART JOURNAL PAGE WITH LOVELY LADY

I also created this page in my art journal with PanPastel. As I normally do, I worked from background to foreground and from top to bottom, and fixed the intermediate layers with fixative. After creating an initial layer for the background, I applied VersaMark over a stencil from my self-designed Pronty Crafts stencil line. I then dabbed PanPastel over the inked area. After that I coloured in the leaves. I created an image of a Lovely Lady on another sheet using acrylic paint and a stencil. I coloured her with PanPastel: I used a good circle stencil to create a beautiful print pattern for her dress. After fully colouring the lady, I fixed the whole thing, I cut her out and stuck her in my art journal. I finished the page with a border of squares. PanPastel's special properties and bright intense colours make it a perfect medium for use in your art journal!

PROJECT:
Colouring page

On page 39 you filled in a colour wheel with the basic colours. I only used cool basic colours in the colouring page of this project. I coloured the background of this picture, from my Tropical Coral Reef Colouring book, with white and blue. PanPastel is excellently suited for use in colouring books: PanPastel adheres well despite how smooth the paper is. Make sure you do not forget to fix the whole thing after you finish, to protect it. I worked from top to bottom to avoid smudging the coloured area with my hand. I then started working on the fish after creating a light blue background. I created various shades of orange by mixing yellow and red together. I used a little violet to suggest shadows on the fish and also revealed their scales. I then passed an electric eraser over the white surfaces on the fish, to reveal their radiant whiteness. I placed a piece of paper under my hand to prevent it from smudging any PanPastel from the surface.

Work from light to dark in the same way as you would paint with watercolours. I applied colour to this picture in layers, using darker colours for each layer in order to create contrasts.

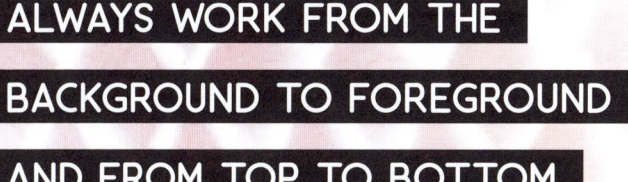
ALWAYS WORK FROM THE BACKGROUND TO FOREGROUND AND FROM TOP TO BOTTOM

PROJECT: GREYSCALE

PanPastel can also be used to colour black and white photographs beautifully. In the days before colour photography, this method was used to hand colour photographs. Using inks, photographs were "colourised". PanPastel is excellently suited to add colour to greyscale prints or black and white copies. The pictures already contain all the grey tones and shaded gradations, so all you need to do is add a colour layer. You will see how I have added colour to a portrait in the examples in the pages that follow. I applied very thin layers of colour to the smooth paper. Start applying the lightest skin tones and then use increasingly darker colours. This is very similar to an ordinary colouring page, extremely enjoyable!

APPLY THIN TRANSPARENT LAYERS OF COLOUR TO SMOOTH PAPER

Practice on these pages by colouring with Pan Pastel on the greyscale portrait and on the black and white photo of the bird

PROJECT: SKETCHES

Earlier on, we made sketches only using black and white. In this project, I will show you how to use PanPastel for sketching in colour. In this example, I sketched the outlines of the flowers on PastelMat paper using a Derwent pastel pencil. Then, I used the Sofft tools to add various shades of PanPastel. This project shows you how easy it is to use PanPastel in a fast manner as well. Try copying these flowers yourself. You can freehand, or use the gridded drawing system: place a grid of small squares (drawing grid) on the photo and on your paper. This way you can copy the image square by square in the correct proportions.

PROJECT:
TULIP IN PRIMARY COLOURS

For this project, I used my basic palette of colours which I showed you on page 37. I started by making a sketch on Canson Mi-Teintes Touch paper. If you like working on other types of textured pastel paper, such as Pastelmat, you can of course use those too. Use your favorite paper!

After I made the sketch, I started applying red and yellow. I didn't mix these directly on the paper, I mixed them first on a large Sofft Sponge. Using the sponge as a kind of palette, on which I mixed the colours. This helps you create a large variety of different colours with just a few PanPastel colours.

It would of course be wonderful to have all 80 colours, but you can also start with some basic colours and then expand your collection of colours.

I juxtaposed the red and yellow tones on the paper. Then I used my electric eraser to "subtract" colour, restoring some of the light back into the picture. I noticed that some of the areas of colour needed a little touching up in places.

I used a kneaded eraser to achieve this. This allows you to generate colour gradations and add more

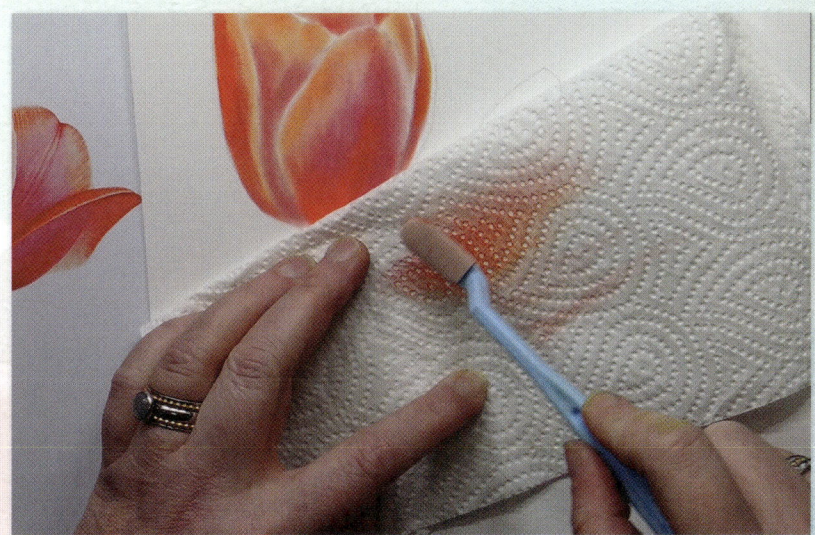

LIFT COLOUR, TO CREATE HIGHLIGHTS, USING A KNEADED ERASER

white to your drawing. Using an eraser allows you to apply light colours over dark ones and make your drawing lighter. I feel it is better to mix your own colours because PanPastel enables this, compared to pastel sticks, it means you need less working space and it also greatly reduces the amount of dust generated on the drawing (and in my studio as well!).

After I was satisfied that my petals were just right, I was now ready to start work on the rest of the drawing. Since I wanted to use different colours, it was necessary for me to first clean my Sofft Tool. It can easily be cleaned by gently wiping it over a piece of paper (kitchen) towel, removing the colour residue.

After that you can easily load a different colour on the tool. I wanted to use a green. Since my basic set does not contain green, I made it myself by mixing yellow and blue. It was very easy: I lifted some yellow on my tool and immediately added a little smear of turquoise. I mixed these

YOUR SPONGE CAN ALSO ACT AS A "PALETTE" ON WHICH YOU CAN MIX A WIDE VARIETY OF COLOURS

colours to a light green on a clean area of my sponge. I also worked from light to dark in the green areas. I used blue from my basic set whenever I wanted dark green. Ultimately, I even mixed black with my yellow and blue mixes, so I was able to create even deeper contrasts and add depth to the drawing. Try making your own design with a limited number of PanPastel colours. This will develop your colour mixing skills.

IT'S GREAT TO BE RIGHT IN THE MIDDLE OF THE VERY SUBJECT THAT YOU WANT TO CAPTURE ON PAPER

PROJECT:
PAINTING OUTDOORS

PanPastel is also excellently suited for plein air painting: painting outdoors. It is very easy to take it outside. I made my own stand for my plein air painting. I use a Heilman Easel® mounted on a tripod, combined with the Easel Butler®. You can see this combination in the pictures shown opposite, which I have copied from PanPastel artist Cheri Ginsberg. This set-up would also work for other mediums & materials. I carefully place my PanPastel on a board. I also fixed my Pastelmat to a board, which I clamp to my easel. You can also suspend a bag full of water bottles on your easel as ballast in case your tripod is insufficiently sturdy or heavy, to ensure that minor gusts of wind do not cause your easel to topple over. You can now begin. It's wonderful to be right in the middle of the very subject that you want to capture on paper!

SKIN TONES

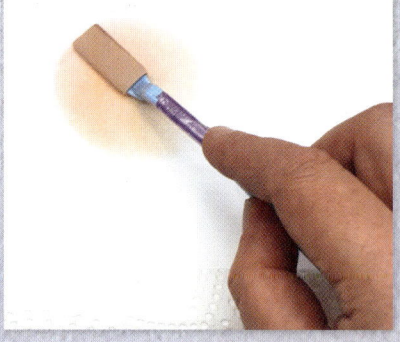

I can use colours from my basic palette to create different tones that I use as skin tones. The Colorless Blender also facilitates colour mixing on the paper. I first double or triple load my tool with different colours. It takes a little practice to figure out how much you will need of each colour, but you can always add a little more. I swipe my Sofft Tools over the PanPastel surface – no rubbing required – it adds enough colour to my tool. When I have the different colours on my tool, I grab some more white and the Colorless Blender and then I mix them together. Of course, there are many colours that you can use as skin tones. The colours I use can be seen in the pictures shown on the next page. If you are working on heavily textured surfaces in particular, it can be easier to use the pre-mixed colours than to mix colours yourself. But with a little practice you can create the same tones using only the basic colours! The PanPastel colours I often use for skin tones are: 660.8 / 780.8 / 580.8 / 220.8 / 270.8 / 430.8 / 740.8 / 470.8 / 380.8 / 340.8 / 270.5 / 470.3 / 780.1 / 780.5 / 740.5

A GENTLE SWIPE WILL GIVE YOU ALL THE COLOUR YOU NEED ON YOUR TOOL

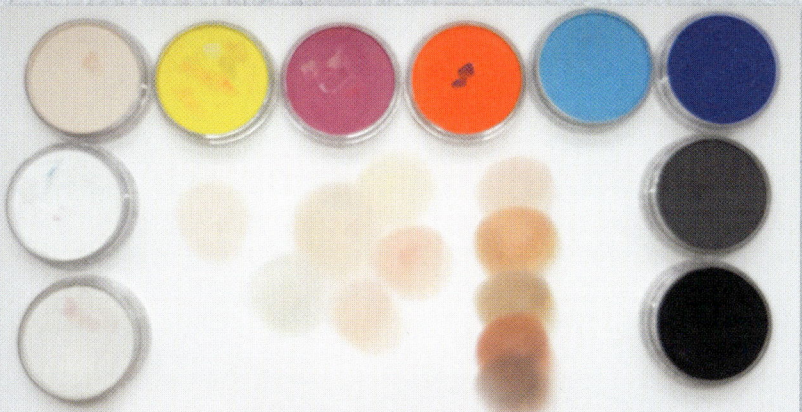

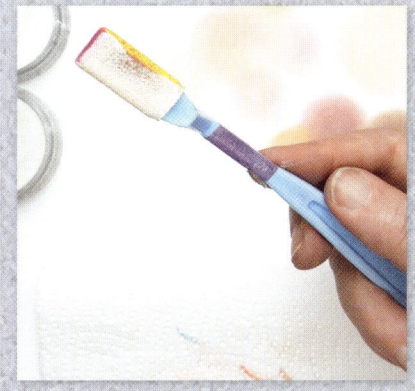

PRACTICING WITH SKIN TONES

In this assignment, you can practice creating different skin tones. I have mixed colours to create different skin tones in the three circles shown.

Circle 1   I started with PanPastel colour Burnt Sienna Tint (740.8). I then carefully placed yellow (220.5) and red (340.5) on my Sofft Tool to achieve a deeper colour.

Circle 2   I then created a darker skin tone by loading my tool with 740.8, 430.5 and 220.5 and added the colours 340.5 and 520.5 and the Colorless Blender.

Circle 3   I used the colours 580.5, 740.8, 340.5 and 520.5 to create an even darker skin tone. To darken the colour even further, I added a shade of grey (820.2).

It is important to practice a lot, so that you get a feel for how much colour you will need. Add some red in case your yellow is too strong. Or add some blue in case your colour is too warm. Try it yourself on the next page. Once you feel like you have mastered it, try it on pastel paper, like the one from Pastelmat. Since the paper is textured, you will find that it grabs more colour requiring more PanPastel and more of the Colorless Blender to achieve the desired result. To make things easier for yourself, you can of course always collect some more PanPastel skin tones as I have shown you on the previous pages.

Practice your skin tones on the next page and write down the colours you have used. This will be useful for reference whenever you want to recreate the colours later!

PROJECT:
PORTRAIT IN COLOUR

I started this portrait with a sketch that I made on dark Pastelmat paper. I used a sponge to apply colour to the large areas. If you want to apply colour gradations, you first have to apply a number of layers. So don't economize on the amount of colour applied, and do use the Colorless Blender. After I applied the basic layers for the underpainting for the face, I used my tool for smaller areas of colour. If your PanPastel underpainting is the right colour, it will make it easier for painting the contours of the face.

After painting the mouth, I went on to develop the eyes a little more. After I was satisfied with the result, I added the finer details with a pastel pencil. This helps create sharp lines, even if there is already a lot of PanPastel on the paper. After completing the face, I started working on the hair. I used different shades to make the blonde hair as lively as possible. I juxtaposed light and dark colours and drew the fine hairs with pastel pencils. The combination of PanPastel and using pastel pencils for the finishing touches, completed the portrait in every possible respect.

USE CONTOURING AND SHADING TO SHAPE THE FACE ONCE THE UNDERPAINTING IS COMPLETE.

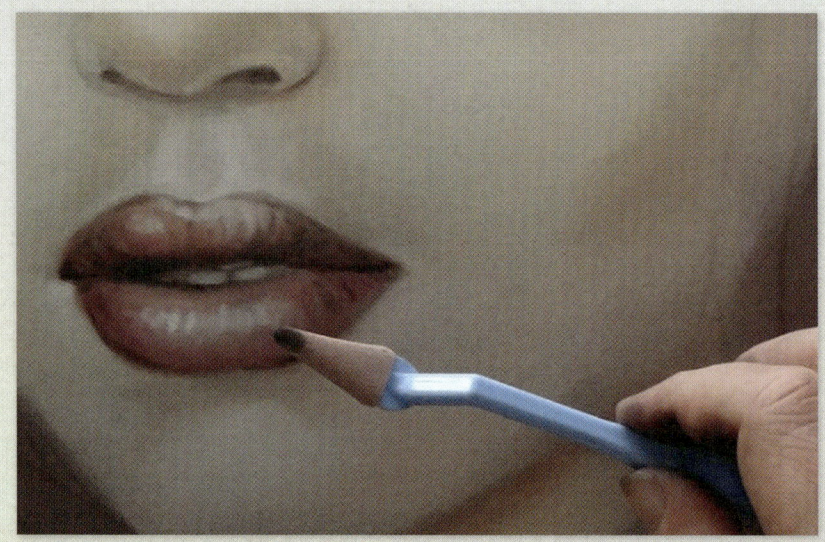

WITH PASTEL PENCILS YOU CAN CREATE VERY SHARP LINES, EVEN IF THERE IS ALREADY A LOT OF PANPASTEL ON THE PAPER

PROJECT: COW

Here I will explain how I painted this cow's head. I chose a medium-light tone Pastelmat sheet for this project. The white of the cow's hair really stands out on the paper. I used the Sofft Tools and a small Sofft Sponge Bar as the image is not very large. If you want to be able to fully mix colours on the Pastelmat paper, then there has to be a good base layer of PanPastel on it. I placed the light and dark colours next to each other again. Make sure you do not put white on top of the dark colours; work from light to dark. I worked in colour groups: first the reddish brown sections and then the white sections. I used different tools for the different colour groups. You can never have enough tools for all your colours! For the background, I used a big sponge and the Colorless Blender. As a finishing touch, I used my tool and sponge to add some extra blue, violet, yellow and pink colours to make the painting playful and lively. I used pastel pencils to add fine hairs, making them look natural.

WORK FROM LIGHT TO DARK

PROJECT:
GOLDFISH

I created this drawing on Pastelmat. I drew from reference pictures and placed the fish together. I was able to use the paper colour for the dark water, which makes the bright colours of the fish stand out nicely. On this paper, you can also clearly see how intense and bright the colours of PanPastel are. I blended different yellow, orange and red tones to paint the fish. I used different tools for the shapes and details on the fish. I used very thin layers of PanPastel in order to make the fins look transparent. Transparency can be suggested by using a dark background. You can do this by building up the fins with very thin layers.

I created the initial sketch with a pastel pencil and used some pastel pencils at the end to add accents. I used a collection of different brands of pastel pencils. I personally like the Derwent Pastel Pencils and the CarbOthello pastel pencils by Stabilo.

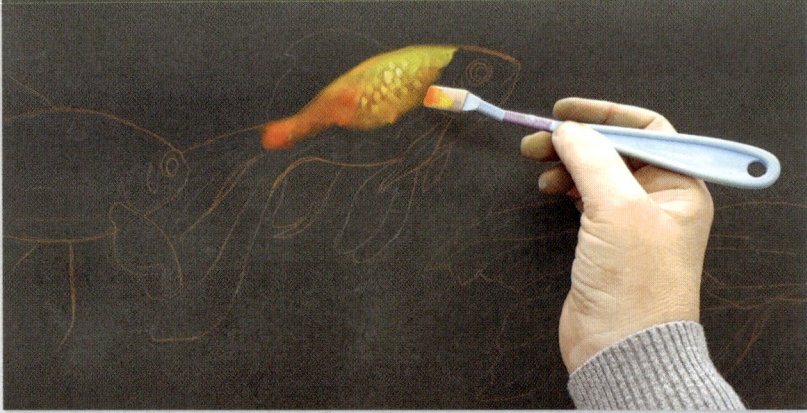

BUILD UP THE FINS PROGRESSIVELY USING THIN TRANSPARENT LAYERS

PROJECT:
LANDSCAPE
A beautiful project with beautiful colours

I developed this landscape using a reference photo. I started at the top and worked my way down. I applied sufficient amounts of PanPastel with the help of the Sofft Tools. Don't skimp on material when applying PanPastel and the Colorless Blender; by having sufficient material on the paper it helps the colours "flow" even more smoothly. I placed light and dark colours next to each other and excluded the parts that were to be made light. After I applied blue for the sky and violet for the mountains, I started working on the warm yellow, red and brown tones. By first making a sketch, I could clearly see where I wanted the colours to be placed. At the end, I added a few details with pastel pencils. I added some swipes of blue PanPastel. The contrast with the warm colours gives the painting dimension, so that it stands out from the paper!

APPLYING PLENTY OF PANPASTEL AND COLORLESS BLENDER WILL HELP THE COLOURS FLOW

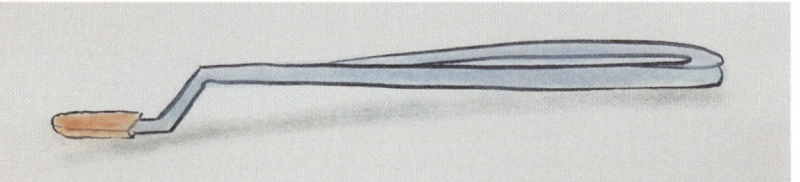

THE BLUE MAKES
THE LANDSCAPE
STAND OUT AGAINST
THE PAPER

PROJECT:
EYE ON CANVAS

Since PanPastel has excellent adhesion properties compared to pastel sticks, you can use it on a much wider range of surfaces. For this project, I selected a canvas from Museo to work on. After making a sketch with pastel pencil, I applied the initial layers for the underpainting with PanPastel. I applied the colours in layers from light to dark. When I noticed that I could no longer apply PanPastel, I knew that the canvas "tooth" was saturated. I then applied fixative to that first layer and then continued applying colours after it was dry. I repeated this process several times, until I had finally created a realistic view with many tones and colours. You will see that PanPastel works very well on canvas, but it is best to fix between layers. So make sure you work in a well ventilated room or that you spray the fixative outside.

I used these colours in this painting: 100.5 / 280.8 / 380.8 / 340.8 / 740.8 / 280.3 / 280.8 / 580.1 / 580.5 / 580.3 / 580.8 / 620.5 / 620.1 / 680.8 / 340.8 / 340.5 / 340.3 / 560.5 / 520.5 / 560.1 / 380.1 / 800.5 / 010.

PANPASTEL WORKS GREAT ON CANVAS. MANY LAYERS CAN BE BUILT UP BY USING FIXATIVE

BUILD UP & BLEND GRADATIONS IN THE UNDERPAINTING LAYERS

PROJECT:
PORTRAIT ON LARGE CANVAS

After completing the previous project, I thought that I could take this further. I chose a large 120 x 80 cm (48 x 36") canvas and transferred my sketch using a projector. I then started with the first layers of PanPastel in skin tones. I used large sponges and applied several colours. I also used the Colorless Blender, to increase the "flow" of the colours when blending. I tried to generate as many gradations as possible in the first layer, both for the skin tones and for the rest. When I wanted to add colour to the eyes and mouth, I switched to the Sofft Knives. This immediately softened the tone and atmosphere of this work, so that it looked like a fresco. I wanted to try to maintain this look. I worked out the colours for each layer and mixed them wherever necessary. When I was finished, I applied fixative and waited until it was dry before I applied the next layer. I repeated this until the portrait was finished and then applied fixative to the final layer.

ON CANVAS WITH A PALETTE KNIFE & STENCIL
I APPLIED MODELLING PASTE & ACRYLIC PAINT

PROJECT:
ABSTRACT ON CANVAS

In the previous chapters, I showed you that PanPastel works very well on canvas. I was wondering if I could get similar results on a textured surface. To put this to the test, I first used a palette knife and a stencil to apply blobs of modelling paste and acrylic paint. After letting this layer dry for 24 hours, I applied a layer of acrylic primer medium over it. This medium "grabs" the PanPastel Colours. I started adding PanPastel, working layer by layer, and after a while I saw that the "tooth" was becoming full so I applied fixative across the surface. After ensuring that the fixative was dry, I started applying my next layers of PanPastel. I did this over and over, until I felt satisfied with the colours and the contrast between light and dark. I finished off by applying some metallic PanPastel colours to the textured sections. This clearly shows that PanPastel is excellently suited for use on textured as well as smoother pastel surfaces.

WORKING LAYER BY LAYER, I USED FIXATIVE WHEN I SAW THE TOOTH FILLING, TO INCREASE ADHESION

AFTER THE LAYER OF ACRYLIC PRIMER MEDIUM WAS DRY, I STARTED APPLYING VARIOUS PANPASTEL COLOURS

PROJECT:
SCULPTURE BLOCK

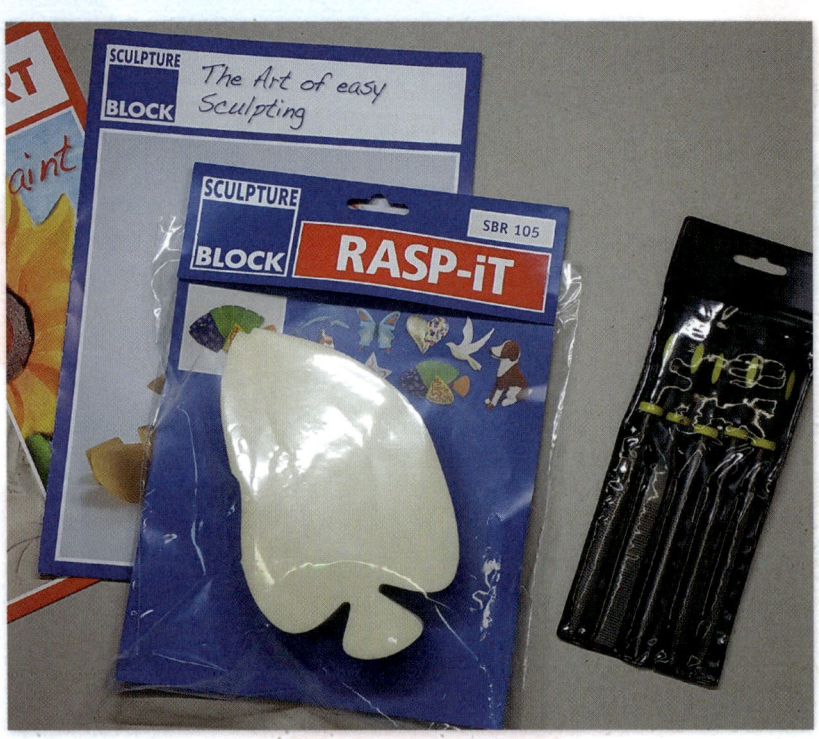

PanPastel can easily be used on a variety of different surfaces. If your working surface doesn't have "tooth" to grab the colour, you can also apply a pastel primer to it. This primer consists of a white, granulated layer, to which PanPastel adheres very well. I used Sculpture Block, which can be used to make sculptures, for this project. Basic form shaped products are also available, in which you are provided with a pre-formed shape and all you need to do is to refine the image. Various kinds of rasps and other tools are available for this purpose. I used the rasp to create the shape of fish that I wanted. That was easy enough, but there was a lot of dust! When I was satisfied with the shape, I used my Sofft Tools and Sponges to apply PanPastel

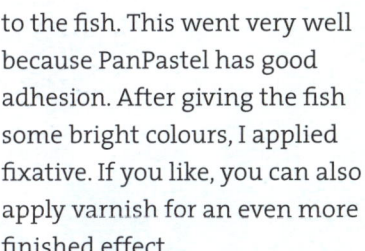
to the fish. This went very well because PanPastel has good adhesion. After giving the fish some bright colours, I applied fixative. If you like, you can also apply varnish for an even more finished effect.

PROJECT:
ENCAUSTIC MEDIUM

I discovered encaustic painting during my experiments with PanPastel: painting with a beeswax based medium. You can make beautiful paintings with an encaustic compatible surface and an encaustic medium. I wanted to create an abstract piece. I heated some medium in a pan (make sure not to over-heat it). Then, little by little, I poured the encaustic medium onto my surface, forming a thin layer. Use a special encaustic compatible surface for this project: it will warp if it is not heat-resistant. After about three layers of the medium, once they had cooled, I started applying PanPastel Colour. PanPastel adheres well to encaustic medium when it is cool, you can easily add colour to your work with your Sofft Tool or Sponge. Then using my heat source to fuse the medium – I used a heat gun as a hairdryer is not warm enough – and a torch is less pleasant to work with than a heat gun. Carefully I went over the work with the heat gun and varied the time that I applied the heat to specific portions. Your PanPastel will fuse very quickly by lightly using the heat gun. But

PAINTING WITH BEESWAX

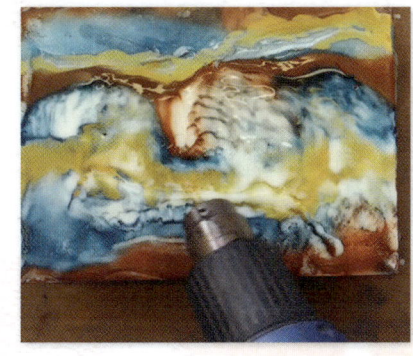

if you apply the heat gun for a longer period of time, the medium will melt and move and the PanPastel Colours will also flow within the medium. Flowing to create waves and shapes that not only look beautiful, but are also fun to make. I then repeated the process: I applied PanPastel and passed the heat gun over it again. I even used a little gold from PanPastel, which produced a stunning effect. Make sure you know what you are doing when you start a project with encaustic medium – it's addictive!

YOU CAN CREATE EXQUISITE PAINTINGS WITH ENCAUSTIC MEDIUM AND A SPECIAL SURFACE

ACKNOWLEDGEMENTS

I would like to take this opportunity to thank my family Ron, Audrey and Rebecca for their support. This has allowed me to do what I love most: drawing, painting, illustrating, designing and teaching. I would also like to thank my publisher Nicole Neven for the confidence she has in me and the opportunities she has given me to make beautiful books for MUS. I would say: may many more books follow.

I would also like to thank Ladd Forsline and Bernadette Ward, founders of Colorfin and inventors of PanPastel, for the wonderful product and tools they have created. In this book, I have tried to demonstrate the wide range of possibilities that PanPastel offers. I hope it has inspired you and I wish you lots of fun in experimenting and creating with PanPastel.

More information about Julia's work can also be found on Facebook, Instagram, YouTube and **www.juliawoning.com/en/**.
More information about PanPastel Colors & Sofft Tools can be found at PanPastel.com and on Facebook, Instagram and YouTube.